HOUDINI

The Life of the Great Escape Artist

by Agnieszka Biskup
illustrated by Pat Kinsella

Consultant:
Carolyn Lane
Curator of Education
The History Museum at the Castle
Appleton, Wisconsin

CAPSTONE PRESS
a capstone imprint

Graphic Library is published by Capstone Press,

151 Good Counsel Drive, P.O. Box 669,
Mankato, Minnesota 56002.

www.capstonepub.com

Library of Congress Cataloging-in-Publication Data

Biskup, Agnieszka.
  Houdini : the life of the great escape artist / by
Agnieszka Biskup ; illustrated by Pat Kinsella.
      p. cm.—(Graphic library. American graphic)
  Summary: "In graphic novel format, explores the life
of Harry Houdini and describes some of his most daring
escapes"—Provided by publisher.
  Includes bibliographical references and index.
  ISBN 978-1-4296-5474-6 (library binding)
  ISBN 978-1-4296-6268-0 (paperback)
  1. Houdini, Harry, 1874-1926—Juvenile literature. 2.
Magicians—United States—Biography—Juvenile literature.
3. Escape artists—United States—Biography—Juvenile
literature. I. Kinsella, Pat, ill. II. Title. III. Series.

GV1545.H8B57 2011
793.809—dc22
  [B]   2010024848

Printed in the United States of America in Stevens Point, Wisconsin.
092010   005934WZS11

Direct quotations appear in **red** on the following pages:

Pages 5, 9, 18, from *Houdini!!!: The Career of Ehrich
    Weiss* by Kenneth Silverman (New York:
    HarperCollins, 1996)

Pages 10, 11, 27, from *Houdini: His Legend and His
    Magic* by Doug Henning (New York: Times
    Books, 1977)

Art Director: Nathan Gassman

Editor: Christopher L. Harbo

Media Researcher: Wanda Winch

Production Specialist: Eric Manske

Photo Credits:
Library of Congress, Prints and Photographs
    Division, 29-31

TABLE OF CONTENTS

b19515923

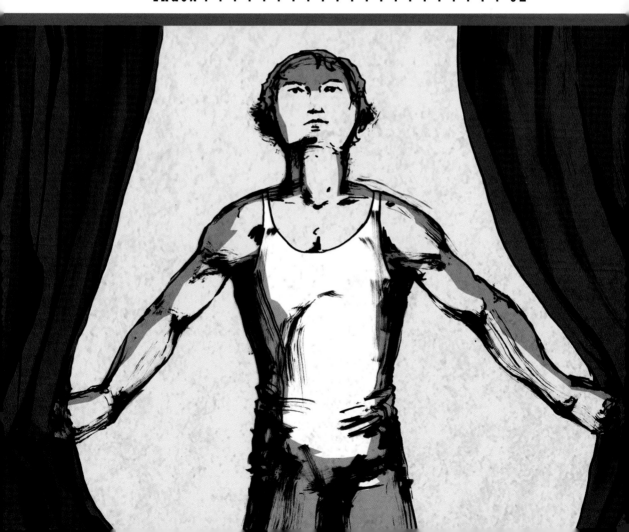

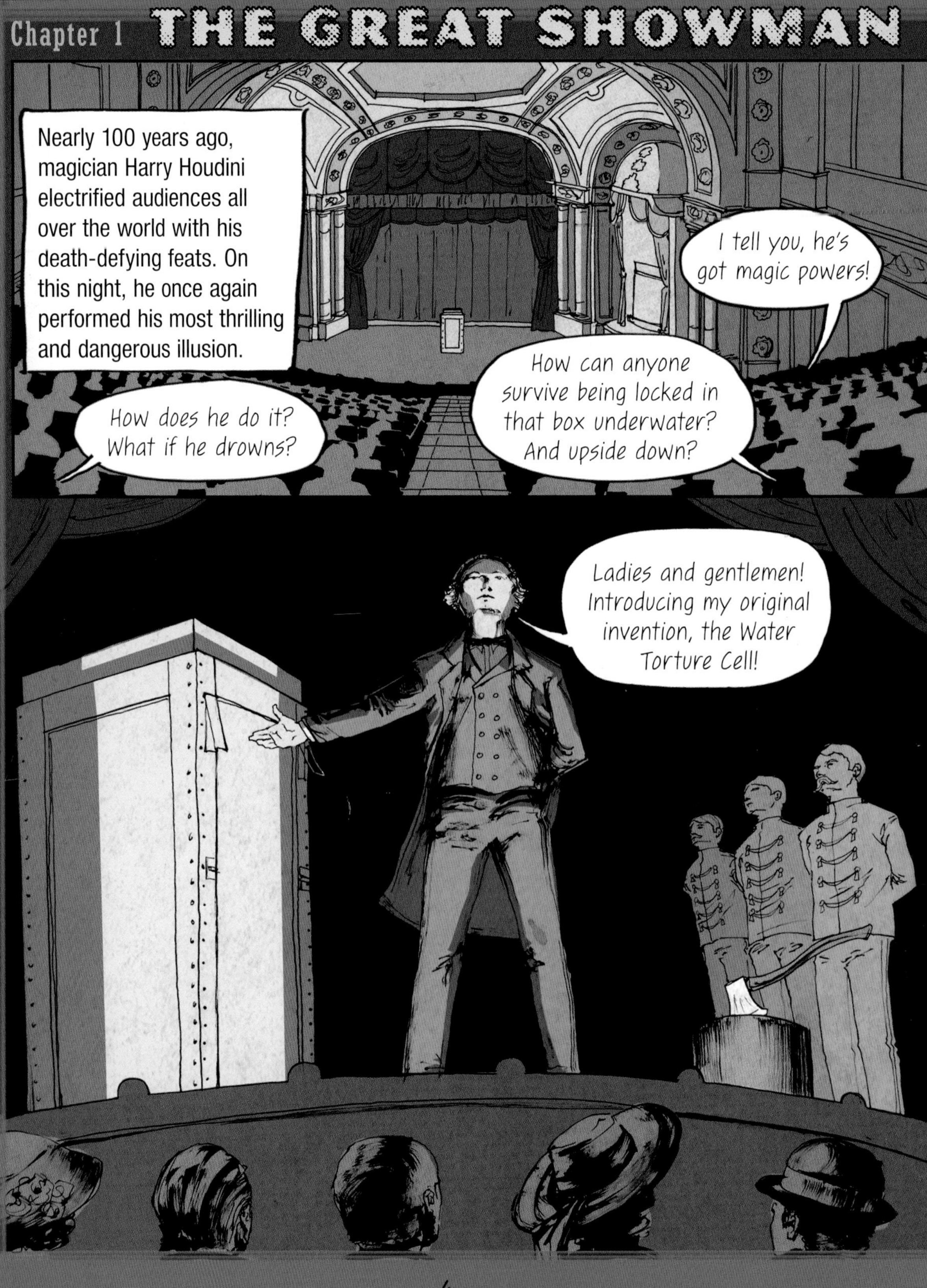

Chapter 1 THE GREAT SHOWMAN
Nearly 100 years ago, magician Harry Houdini electrified audiences all over the world with his death-defying feats. On this night, he once again performed his most thrilling and dangerous illusion.
How does he do it? What if he drowns?
How can anyone survive being locked in that box underwater? And upside down?
I tell you, he's got magic powers!
Ladies and gentlemen! Introducing my original invention, the Water Torture Cell!

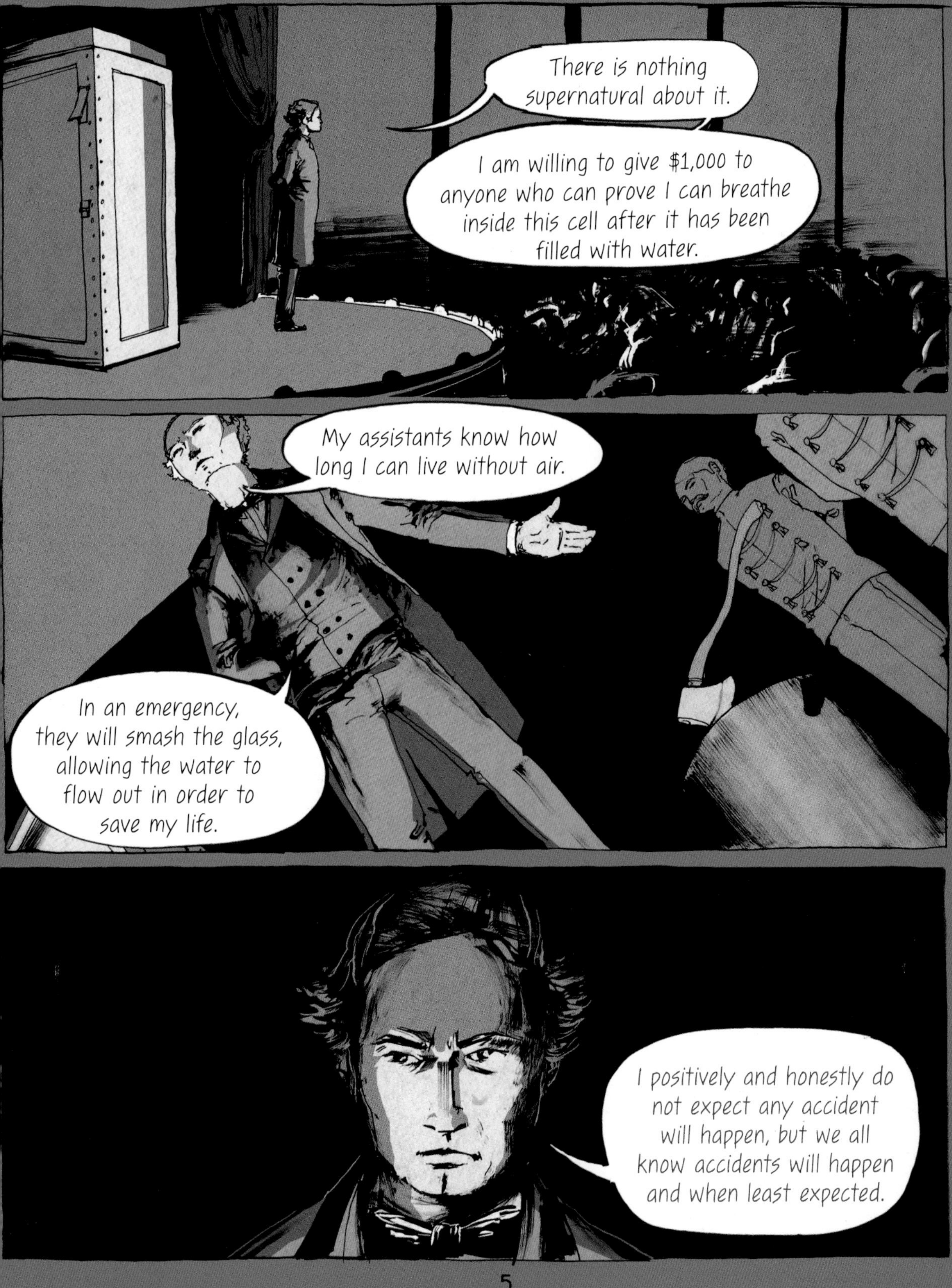
There is nothing supernatural about it.
I am willing to give $1,000 to anyone who can prove I can breathe inside this cell after it has been filled with water.
My assistants know how long I can live without air.
In an emergency, they will smash the glass, allowing the water to flow out in order to save my life.
I positively and honestly do not expect any accident will happen, but we all know accidents will happen and when least expected.

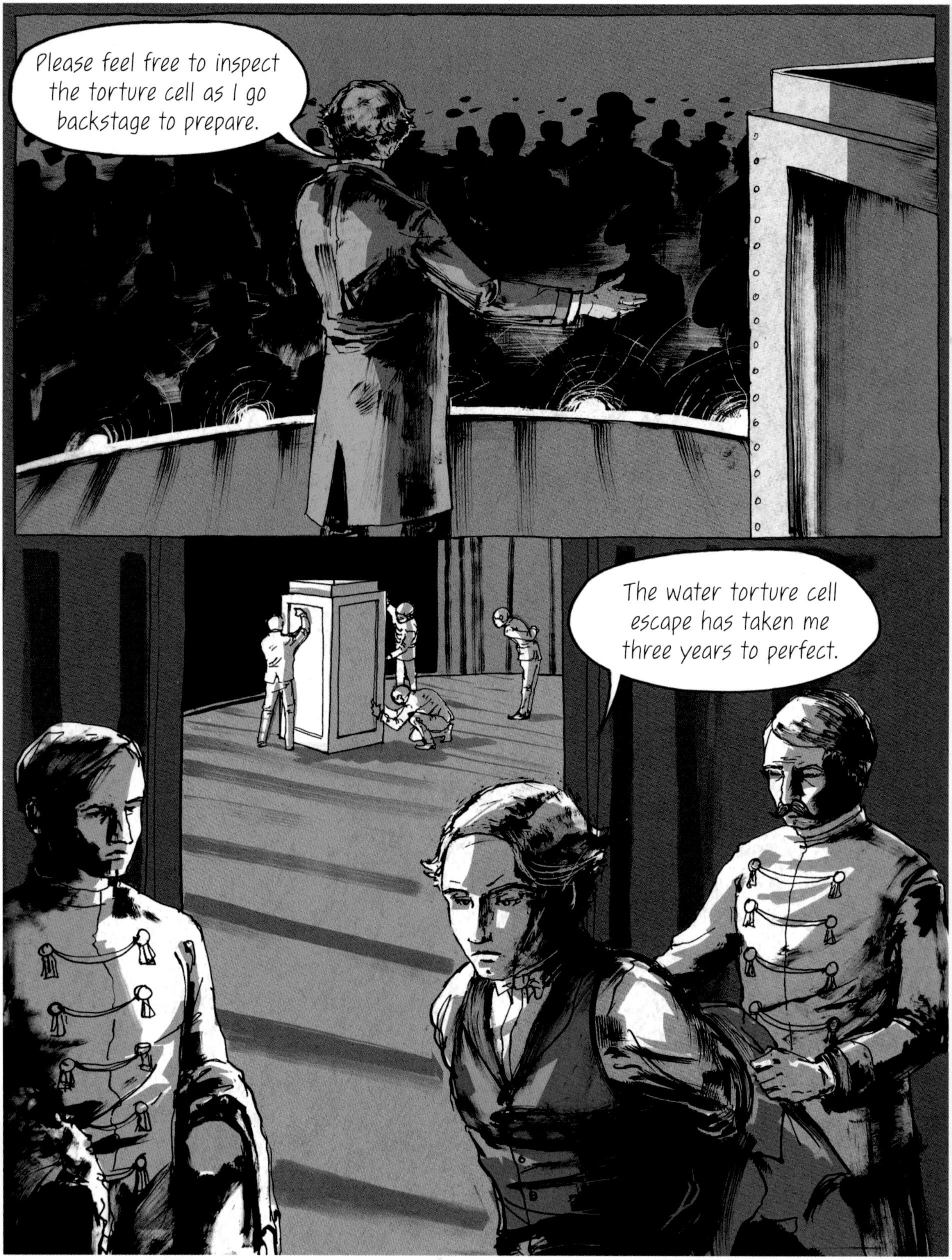
Please feel free to inspect the torture cell as I go backstage to prepare.
The water torture cell escape has taken me three years to perfect.

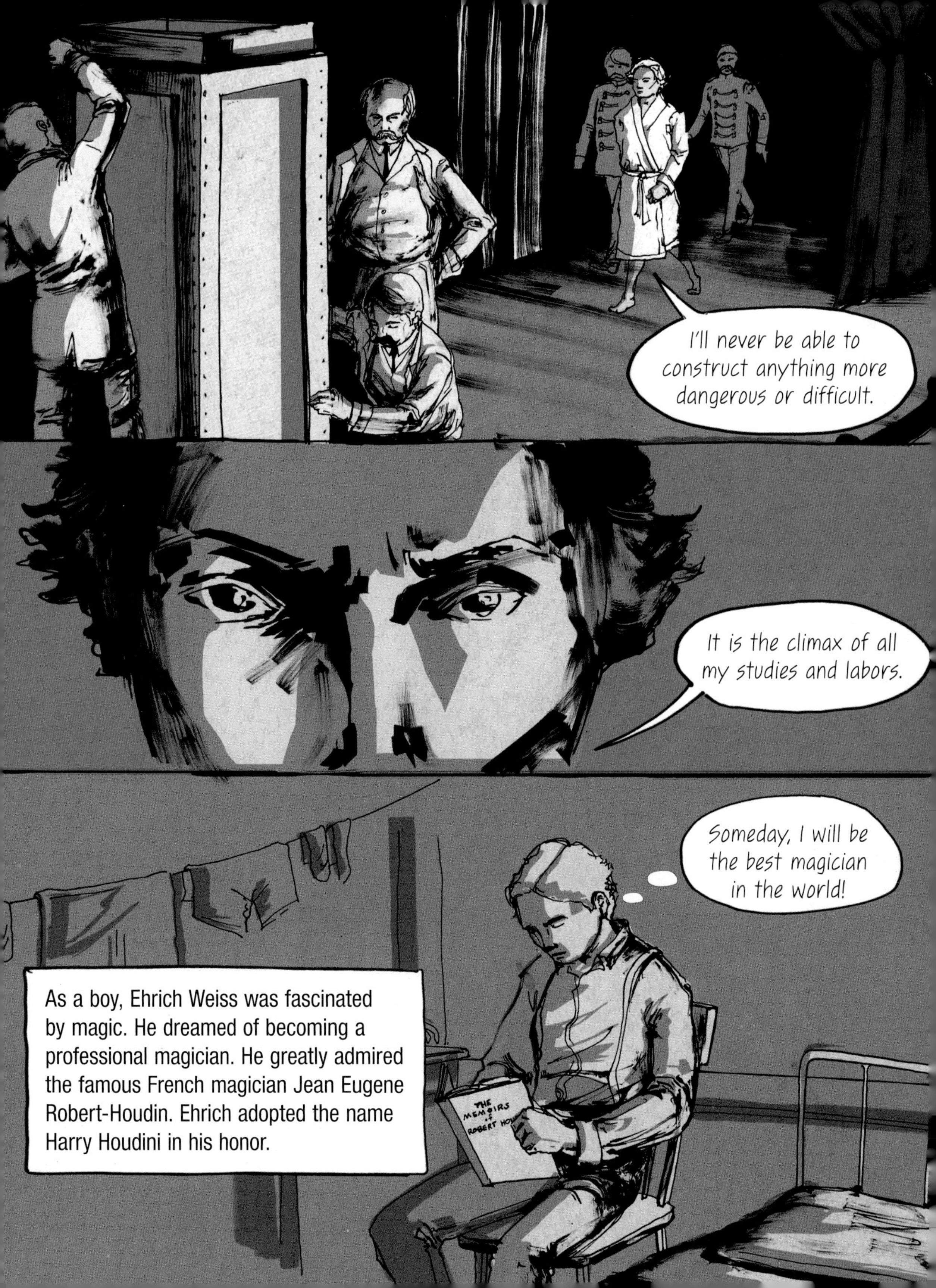
I'll never be able to construct anything more dangerous or difficult.
It is the climax of all my studies and labors.
Someday, I will be the best magician in the world!
As a boy, Ehrich Weiss was fascinated by magic. He dreamed of becoming a professional magician. He greatly admired the famous French magician Jean Eugene Robert-Houdin. Ehrich adopted the name Harry Houdini in his honor.

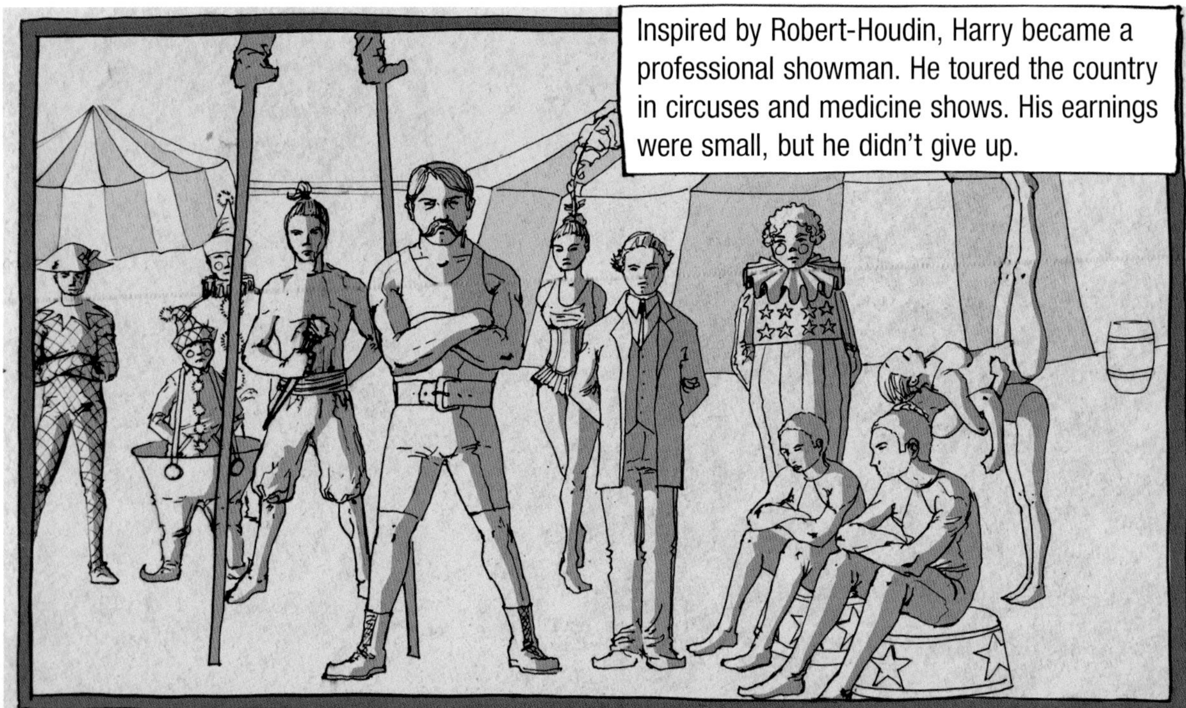
Inspired by Robert-Houdin, Harry became a professional showman. He toured the country in circuses and medicine shows. His earnings were small, but he didn't give up.

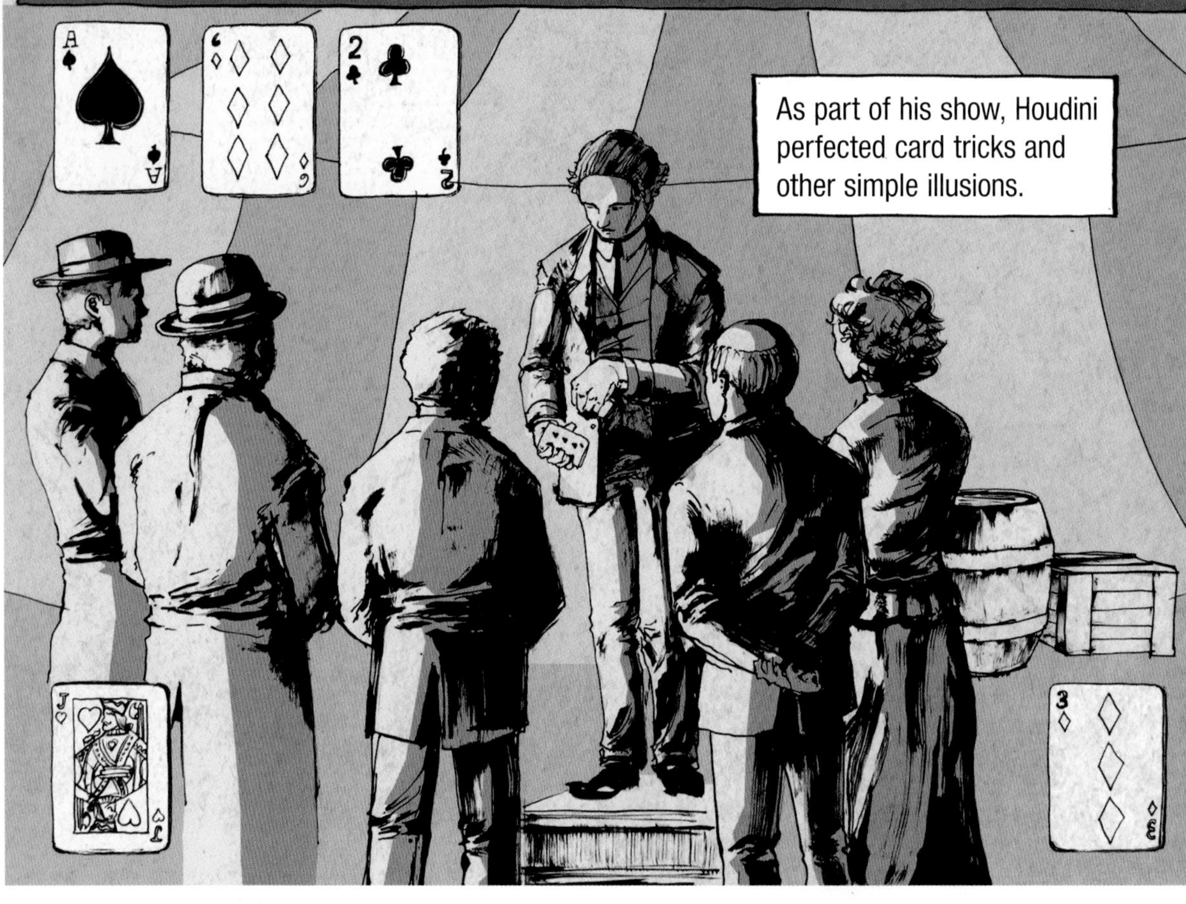
As part of his show, Houdini perfected card tricks and other simple illusions.

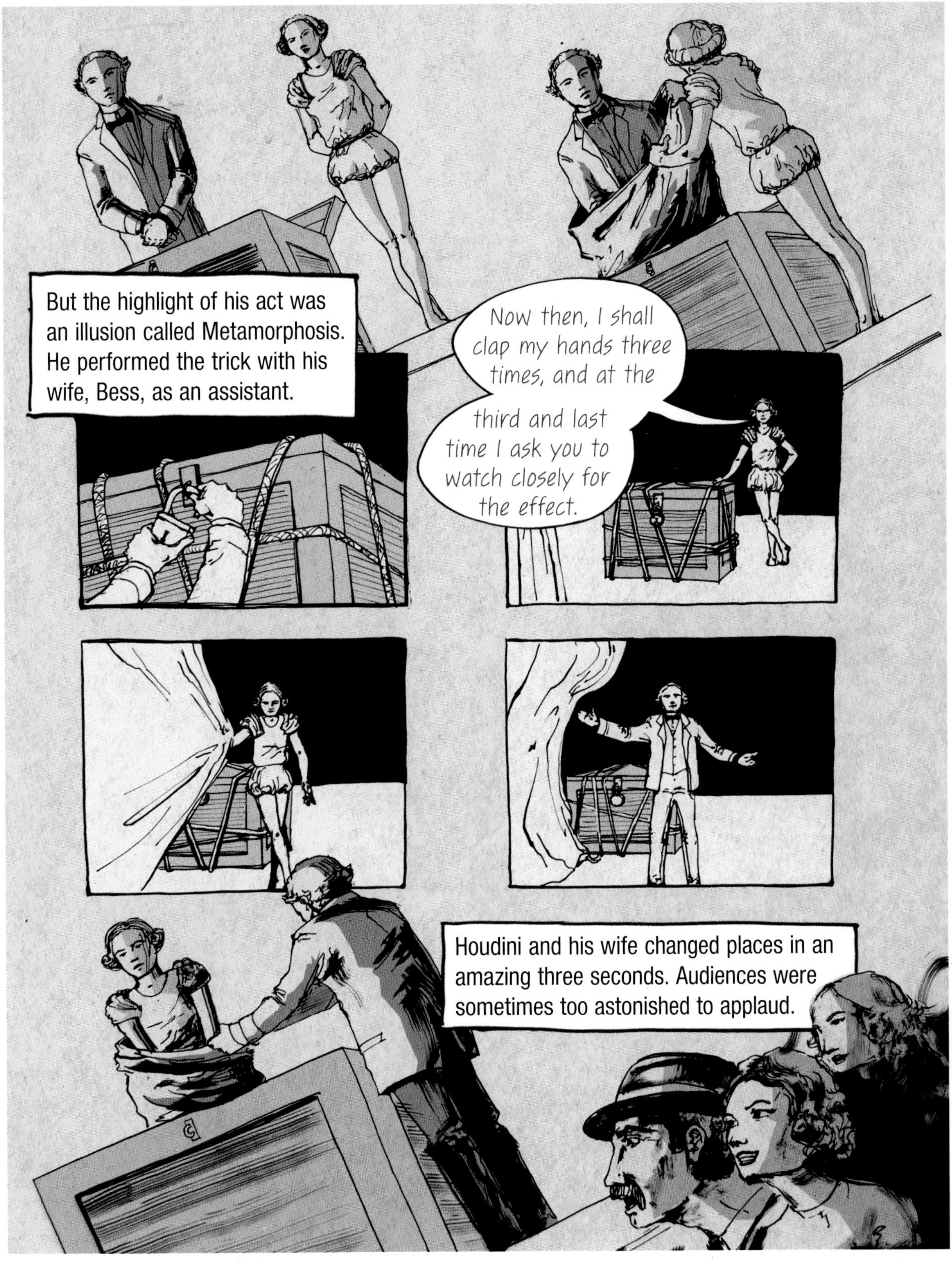

But the highlight of his act was an illusion called Metamorphosis. He performed the trick with his wife, Bess, as an assistant.
Now then, I shall clap my hands three times, and at the
third and last time I ask you to watch closely for the effect.
Houdini and his wife changed places in an amazing three seconds. Audiences were sometimes too astonished to applaud.

Chapter 2 THE HANDCUFF KING

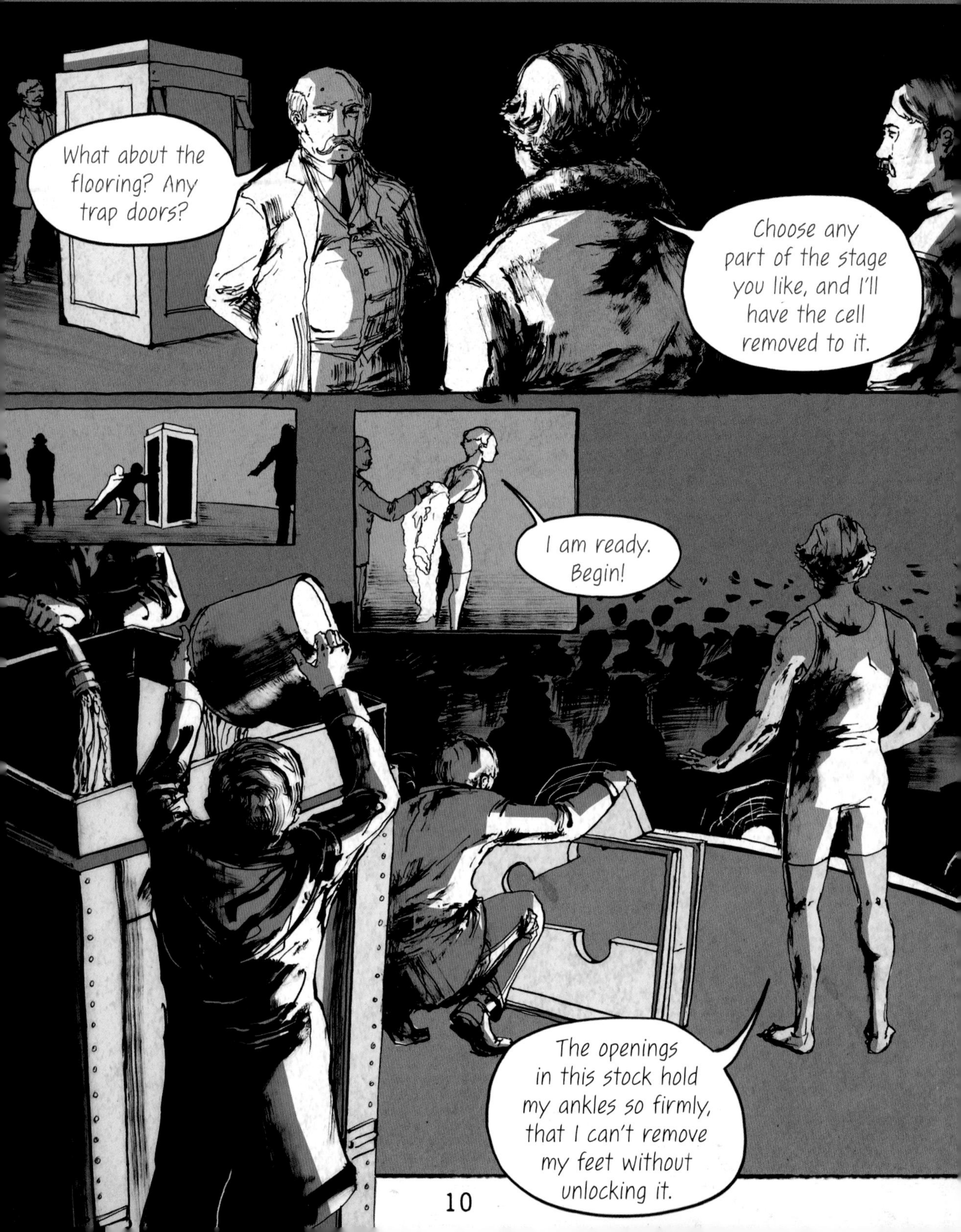
What about the flooring? Any trap doors?
Choose any part of the stage you like, and I'll have the cell removed to it.
I am ready. Begin!
The openings in this stock hold my ankles so firmly, that I can't remove my feet without unlocking it.

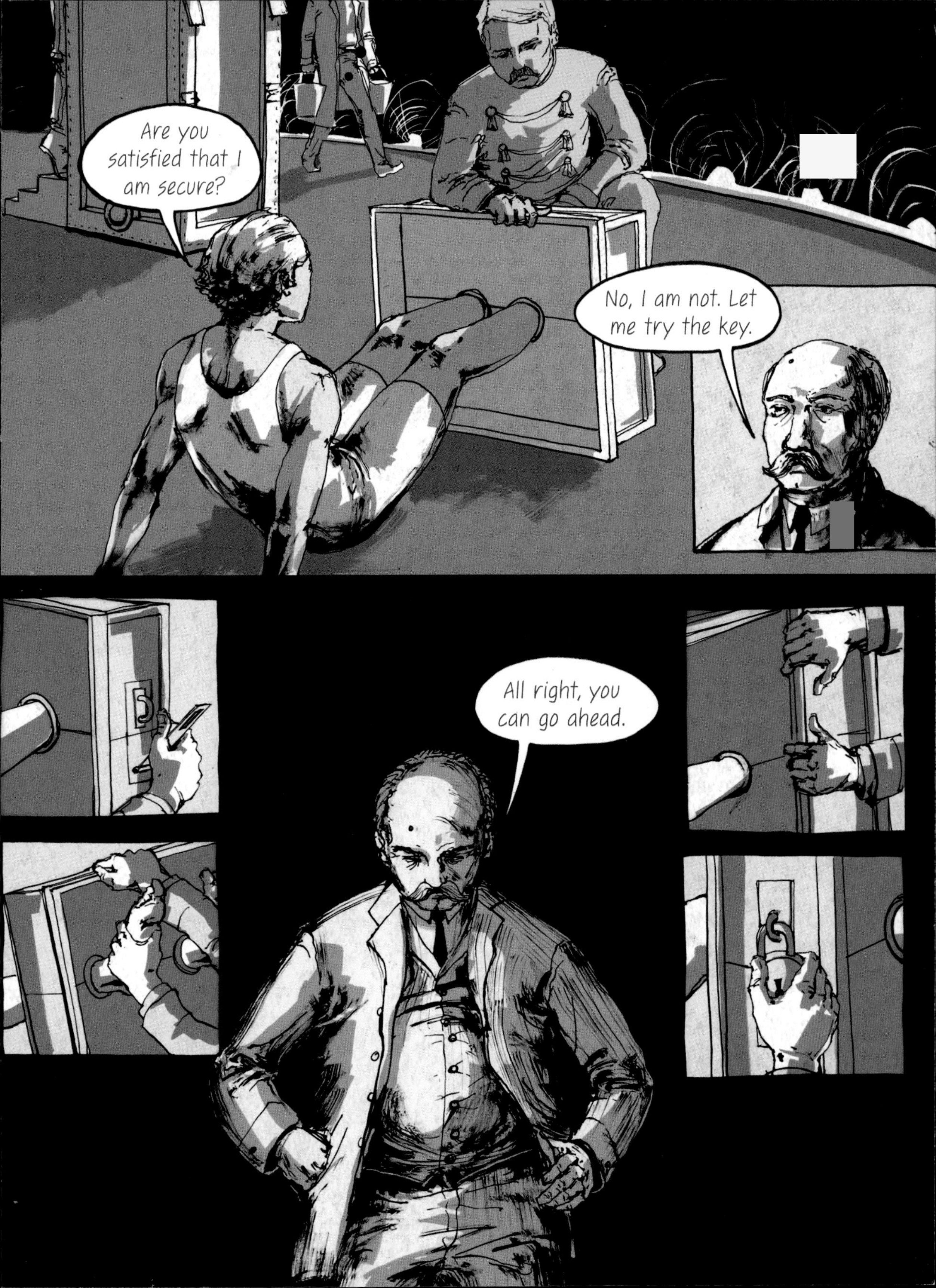
Are you satisfied that I am secure?
No, I am not. Let me try the key.
All right, you can go ahead.

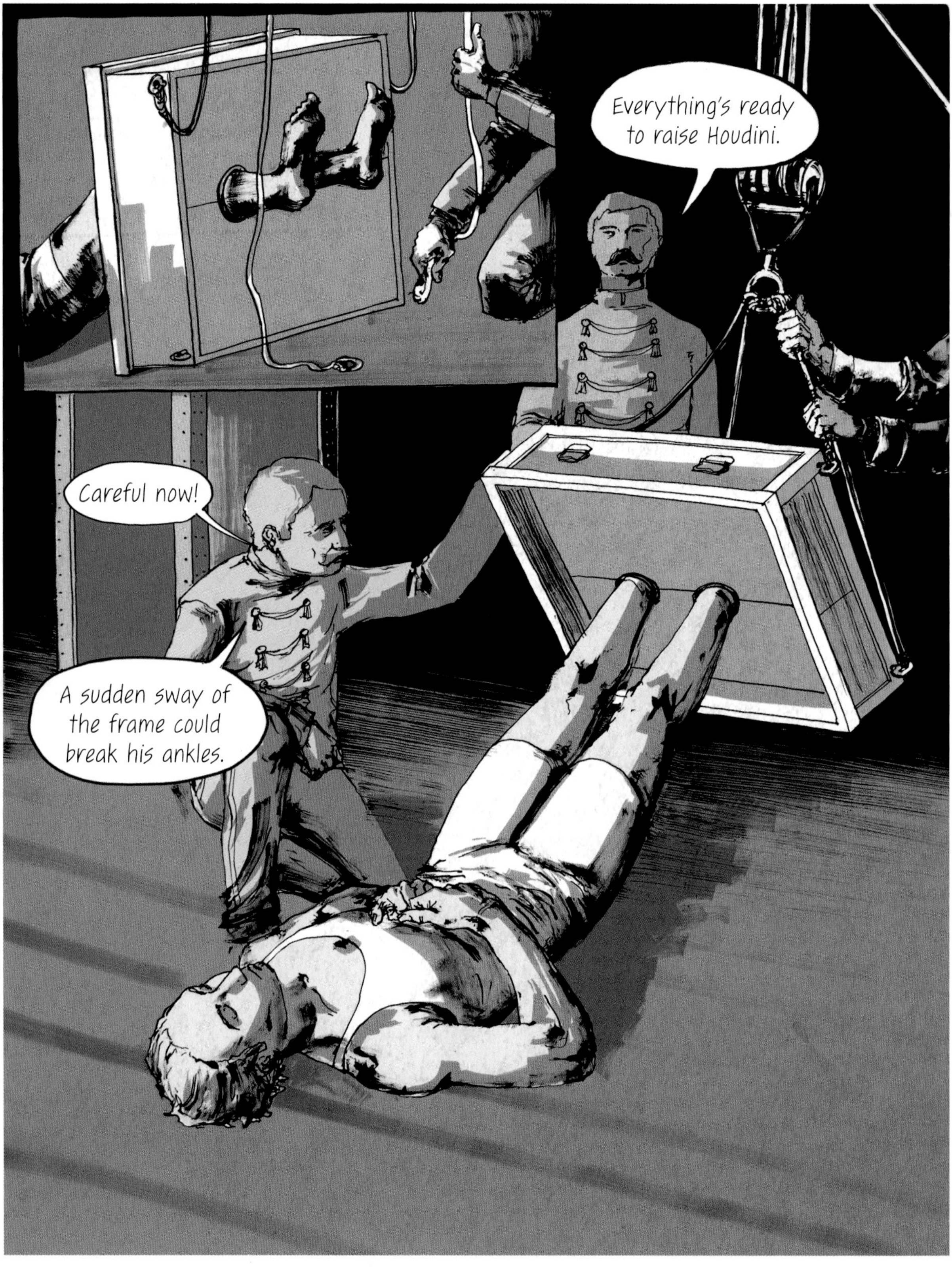
Everything's ready to raise Houdini.
Careful now!
A sudden sway of the frame could break his ankles.

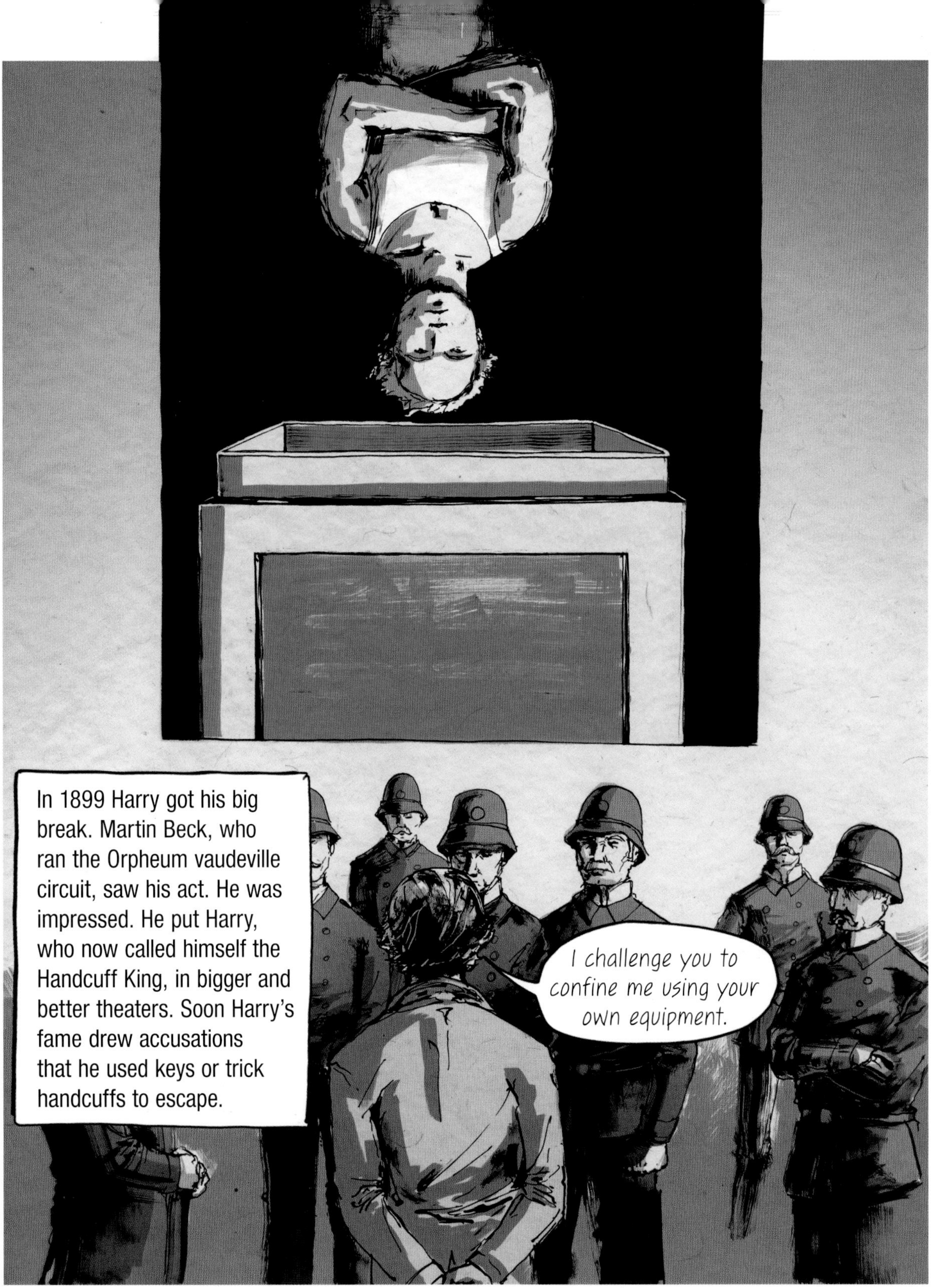
In 1899 Harry got his big break. Martin Beck, who ran the Orpheum vaudeville circuit, saw his act. He was impressed. He put Harry, who now called himself the Handcuff King, in bigger and better theaters. Soon Harry's fame drew accusations that he used keys or trick handcuffs to escape.
I challenge you to confine me using your own equipment.

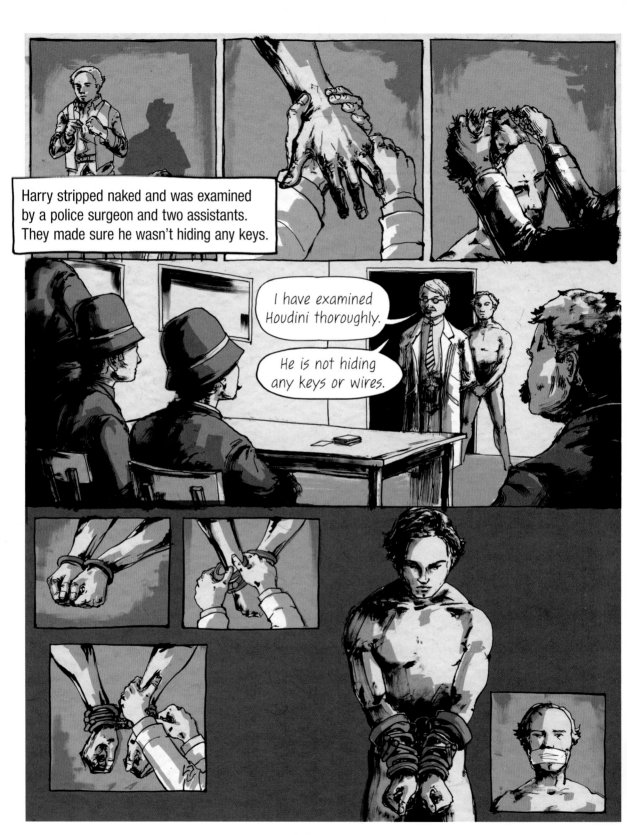

Harry stripped naked and was examined by a police surgeon and two assistants. They made sure he wasn't hiding any keys.

I have examined Houdini thoroughly.

He is not hiding any keys or wires.

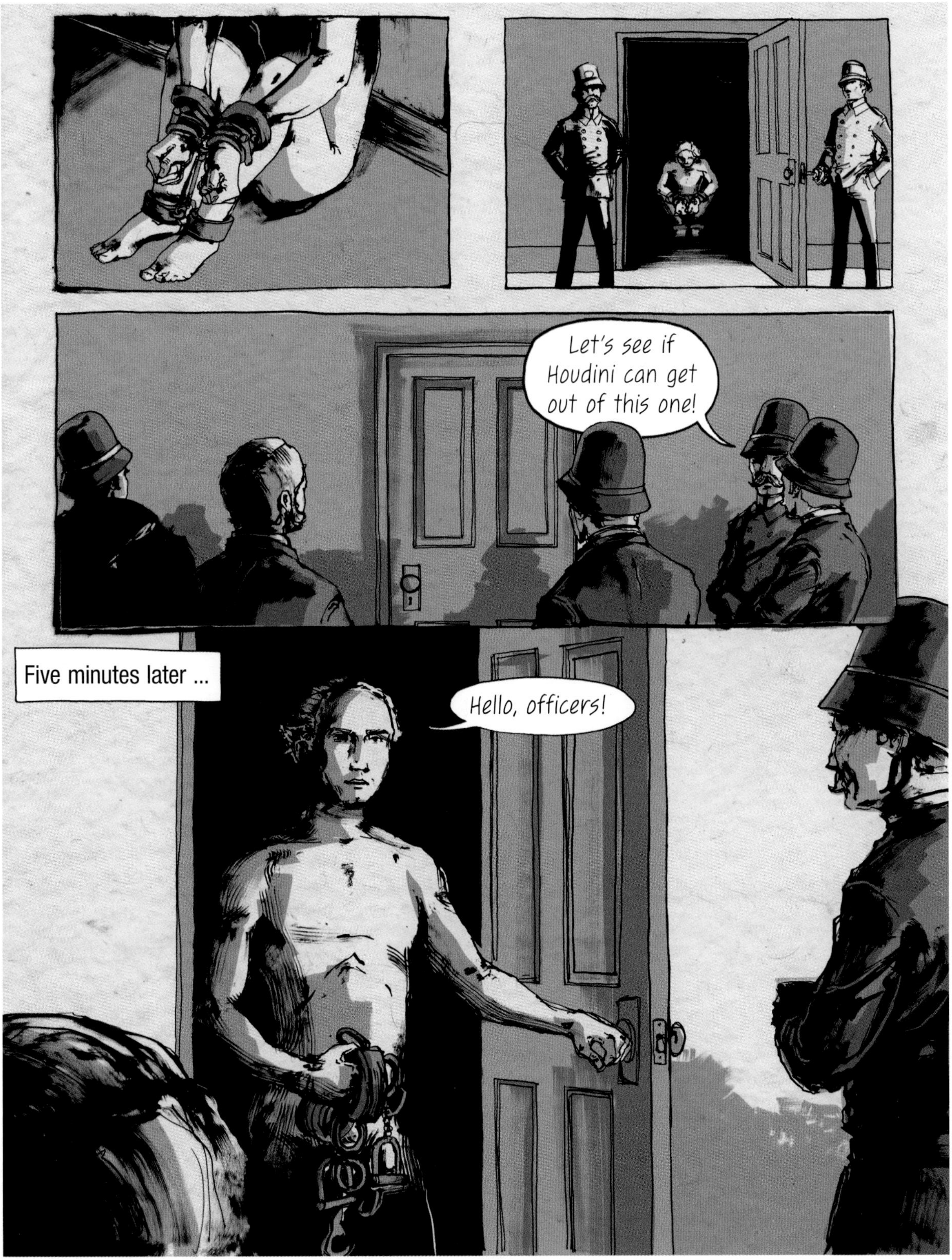
Let's see if Houdini can get out of this one!
Five minutes later ...
Hello, officers!

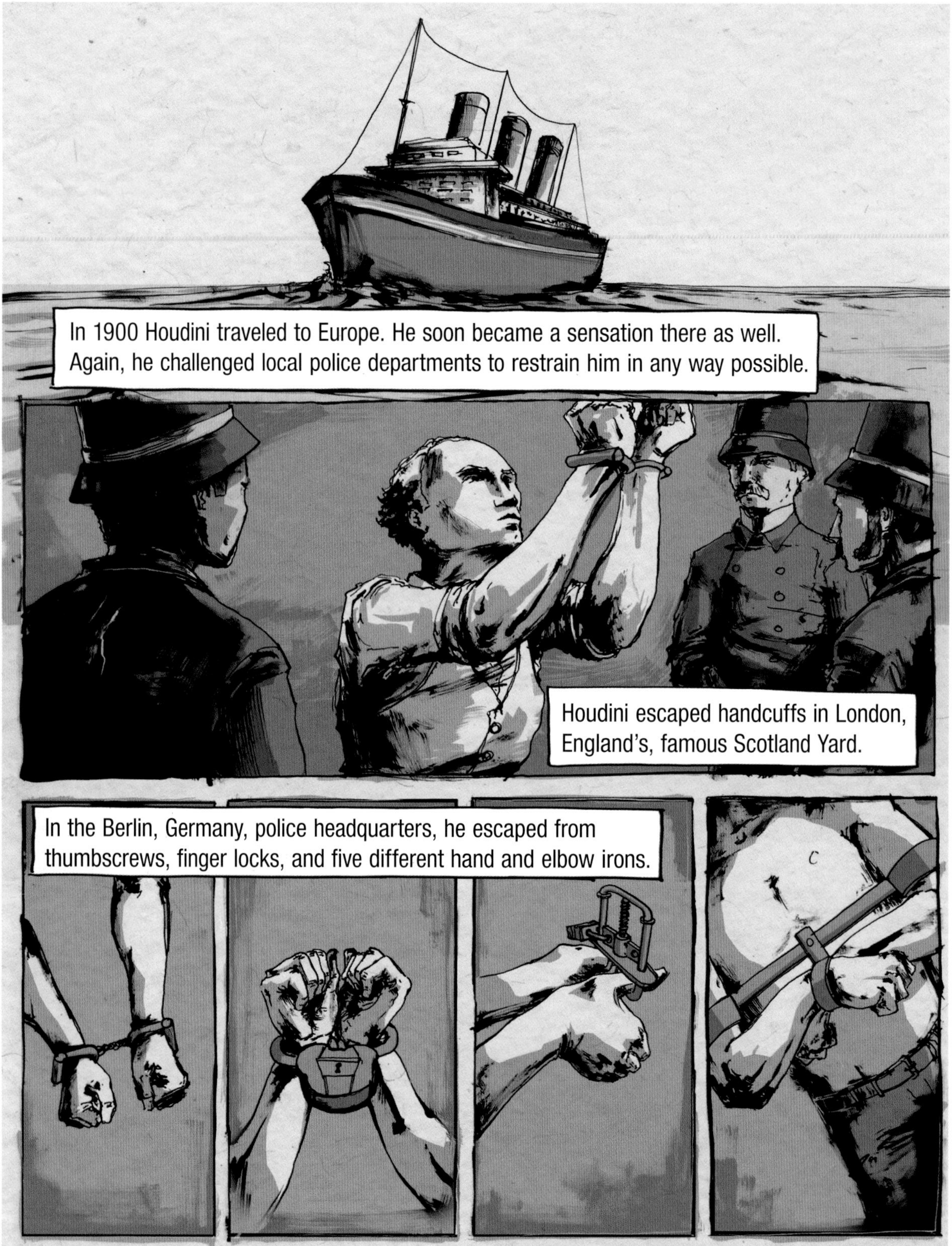
In 1900 Houdini traveled to Europe. He soon became a sensation there as well. Again, he challenged local police departments to restrain him in any way possible.
Houdini escaped handcuffs in London, England's, famous Scotland Yard.
In the Berlin, Germany, police headquarters, he escaped from thumbscrews, finger locks, and five different hand and elbow irons.

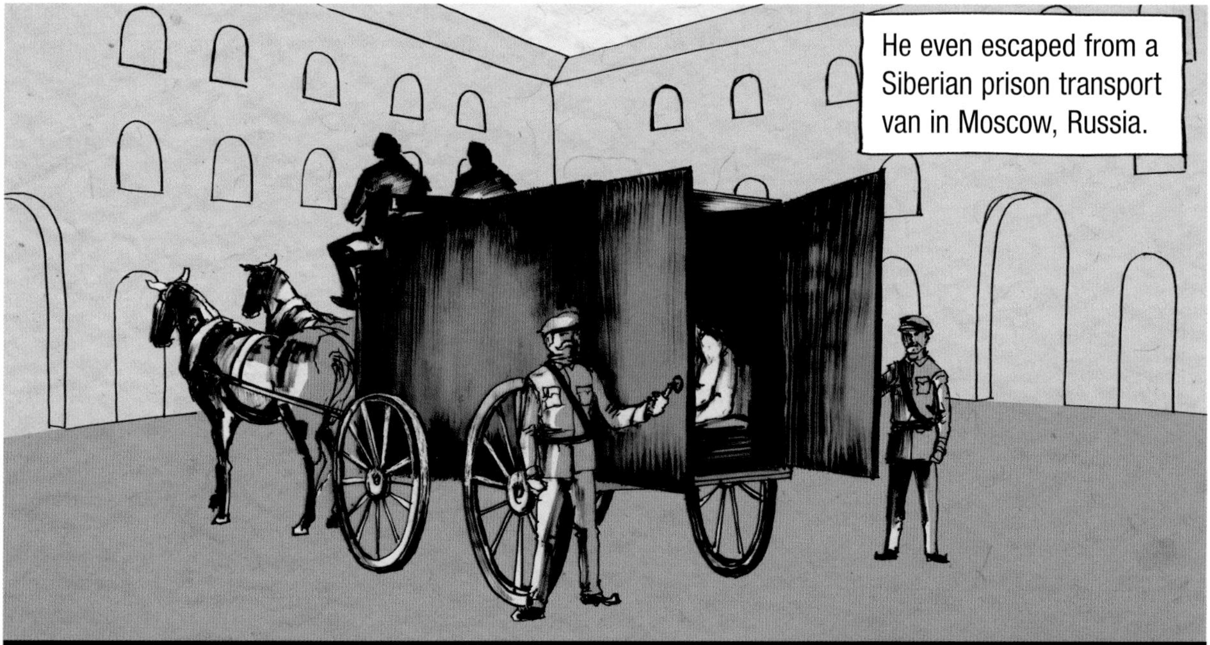
He even escaped from a Siberian prison transport van in Moscow, Russia.

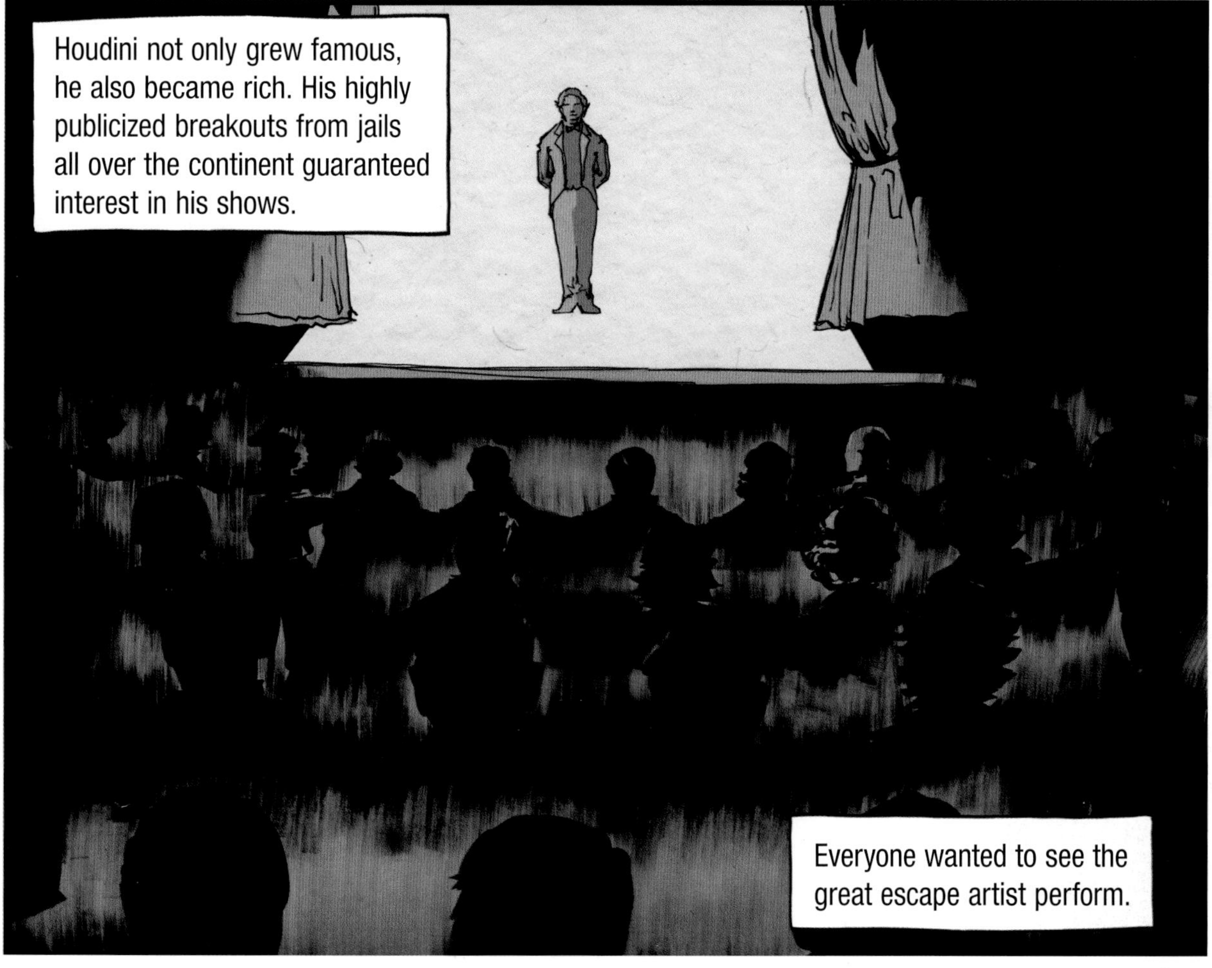
Houdini not only grew famous, he also became rich. His highly publicized breakouts from jails all over the continent guaranteed interest in his shows.
Everyone wanted to see the great escape artist perform.

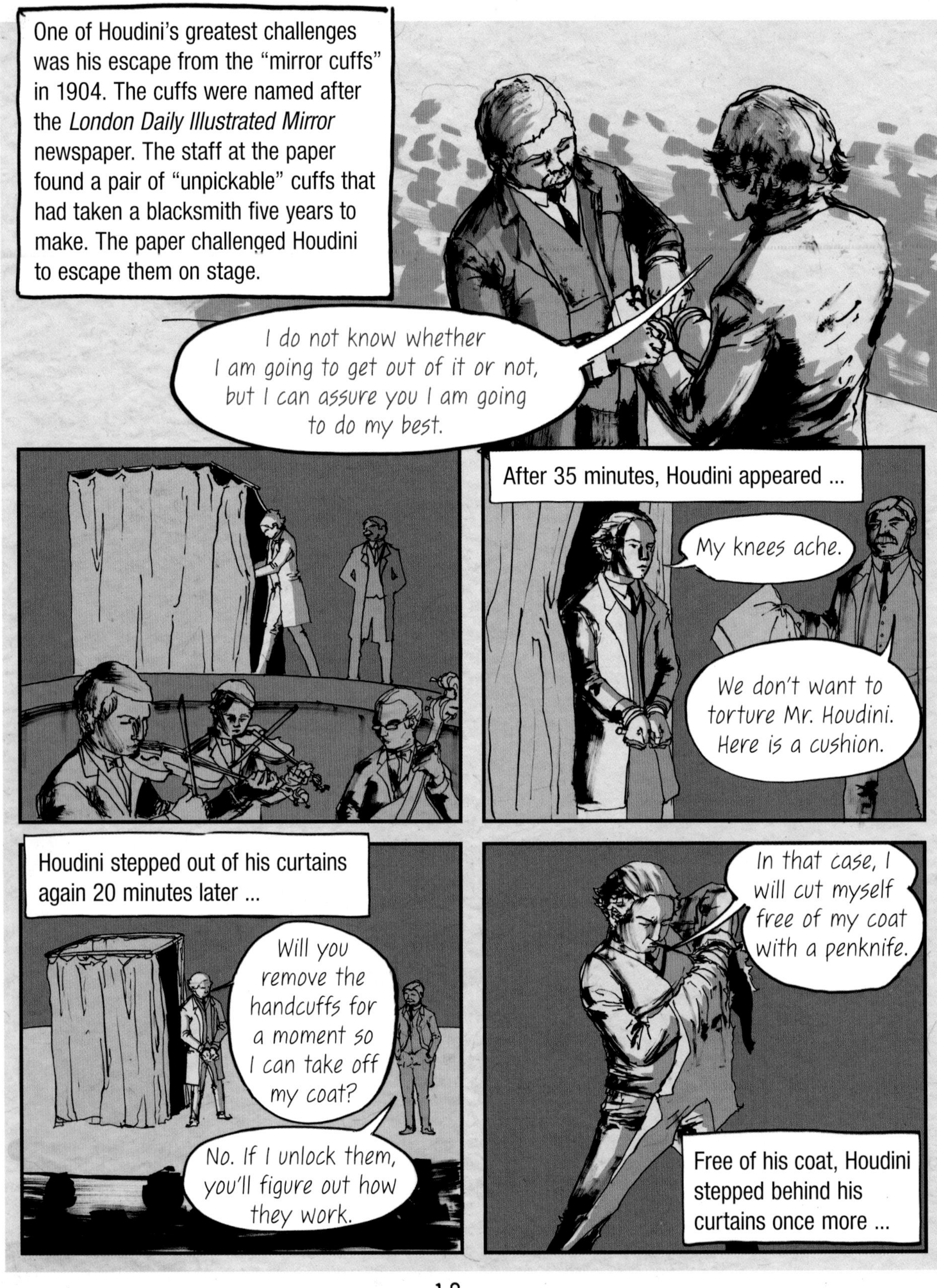
One of Houdini's greatest challenges was his escape from the "mirror cuffs" in 1904. The cuffs were named after the *London Daily Illustrated Mirror* newspaper. The staff at the paper found a pair of "unpickable" cuffs that had taken a blacksmith five years to make. The paper challenged Houdini to escape them on stage.
I do not know whether I am going to get out of it or not, but I can assure you I am going to do my best.
After 35 minutes, Houdini appeared ...
My knees ache.
We don't want to torture Mr. Houdini. Here is a cushion.
Houdini stepped out of his curtains again 20 minutes later ...
Will you remove the handcuffs for a moment so I can take off my coat?
No. If I unlock them, you'll figure out how they work.
In that case, I will cut myself free of my coat with a penknife.
Free of his coat, Houdini stepped behind his curtains once more ...

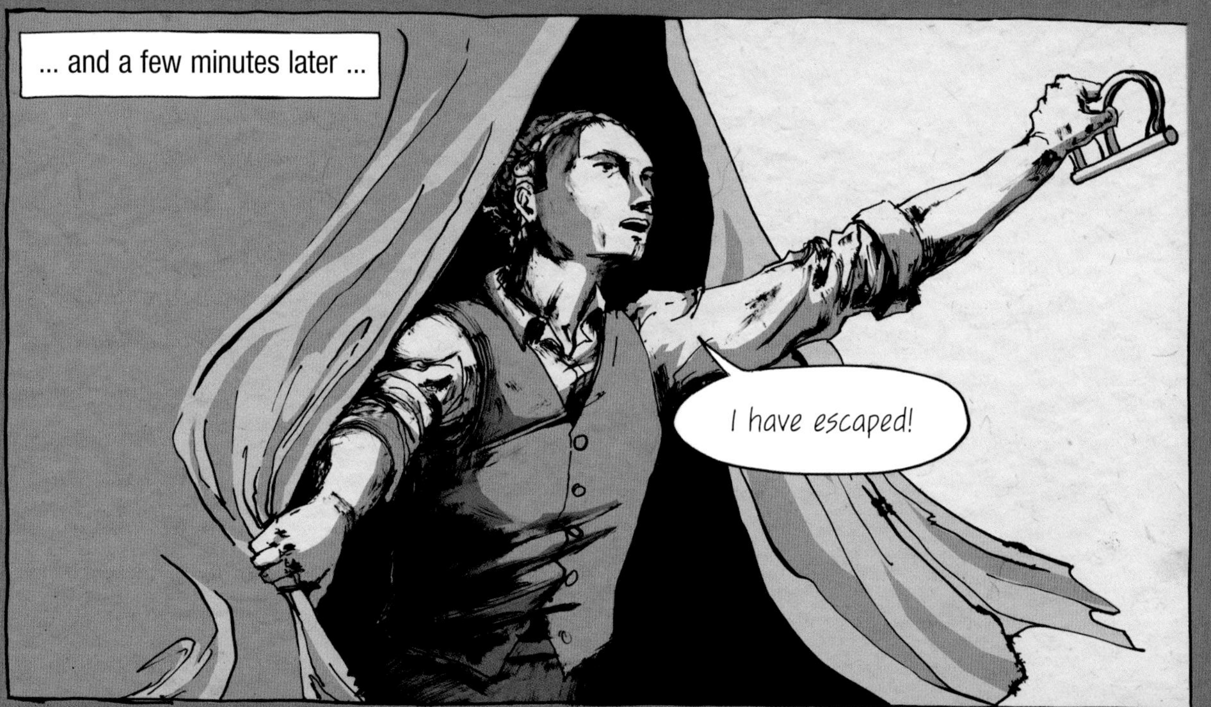
... and a few minutes later ...
I have escaped!

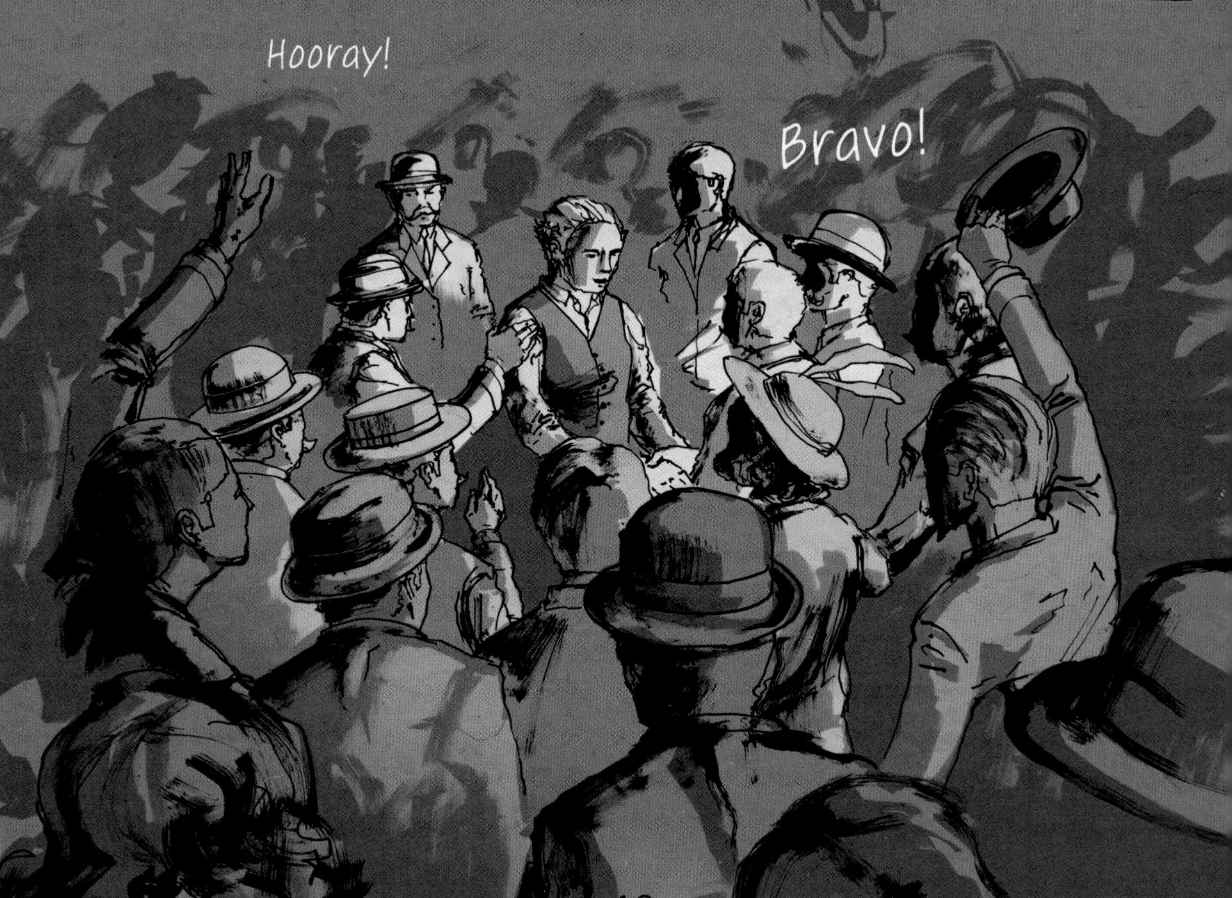
Hooray!
Bravo!

Chapter 3

DEATH-DEFYING ACTS

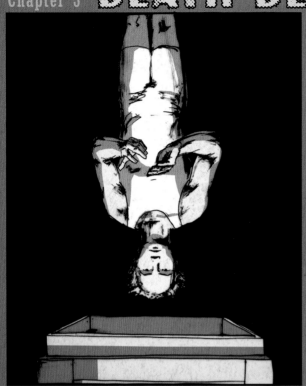

Gracious! He's gone in!

He'll drown if he fails!

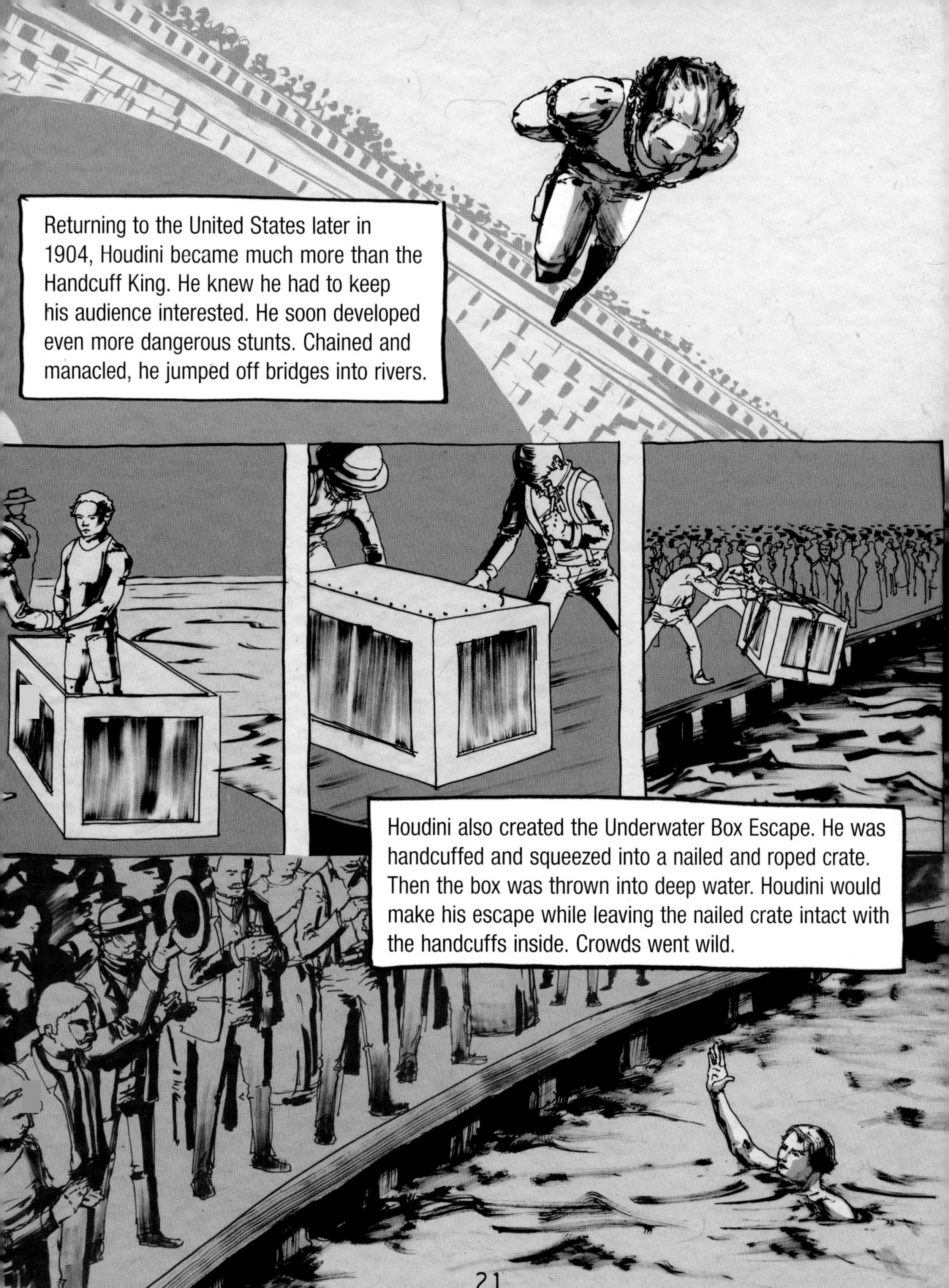
Returning to the United States later in 1904, Houdini became much more than the Handcuff King. He knew he had to keep his audience interested. He soon developed even more dangerous stunts. Chained and manacled, he jumped off bridges into rivers.
Houdini also created the Underwater Box Escape. He was handcuffed and squeezed into a nailed and roped crate. Then the box was thrown into deep water. Houdini would make his escape while leaving the nailed crate intact with the handcuffs inside. Crowds went wild.

Houdini became the world's greatest escape artist. Between 1904 and 1915 he invented many amazing escapes.

CHALL
HOU

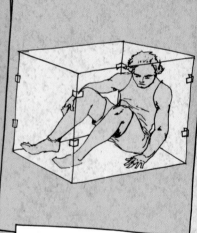

He escaped from a sealed milk can filled with water. He advertised the stunt with the words, "failure means a drowning death."

He escaped a giant sealed paper envelope without tearing it.

A locked glass box could not hold Houdini for long.

HOUDINI
ACCEPTS CHALLENGE

ENGE
DINI

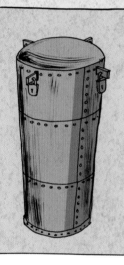

Neither could a boiler that had been welded shut ...

... or a locked mail bag.

Houdini even escaped from a giant football. Was there anything he couldn't escape?

WILL FORFEIT $100
TO ANYONE WHO CAN FIND ANY
FALSE MEANS OF EXITS OR TRAP

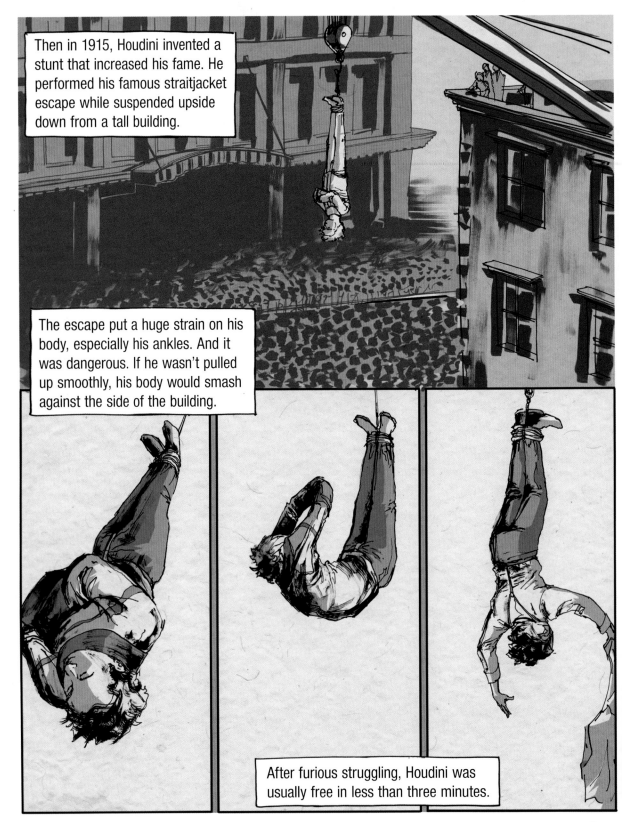

Then in 1915, Houdini invented a stunt that increased his fame. He performed his famous straitjacket escape while suspended upside down from a tall building.

The escape put a huge strain on his body, especially his ankles. And it was dangerous. If he wasn't pulled up smoothly, his body would smash against the side of the building.

After furious struggling, Houdini was usually free in less than three minutes.

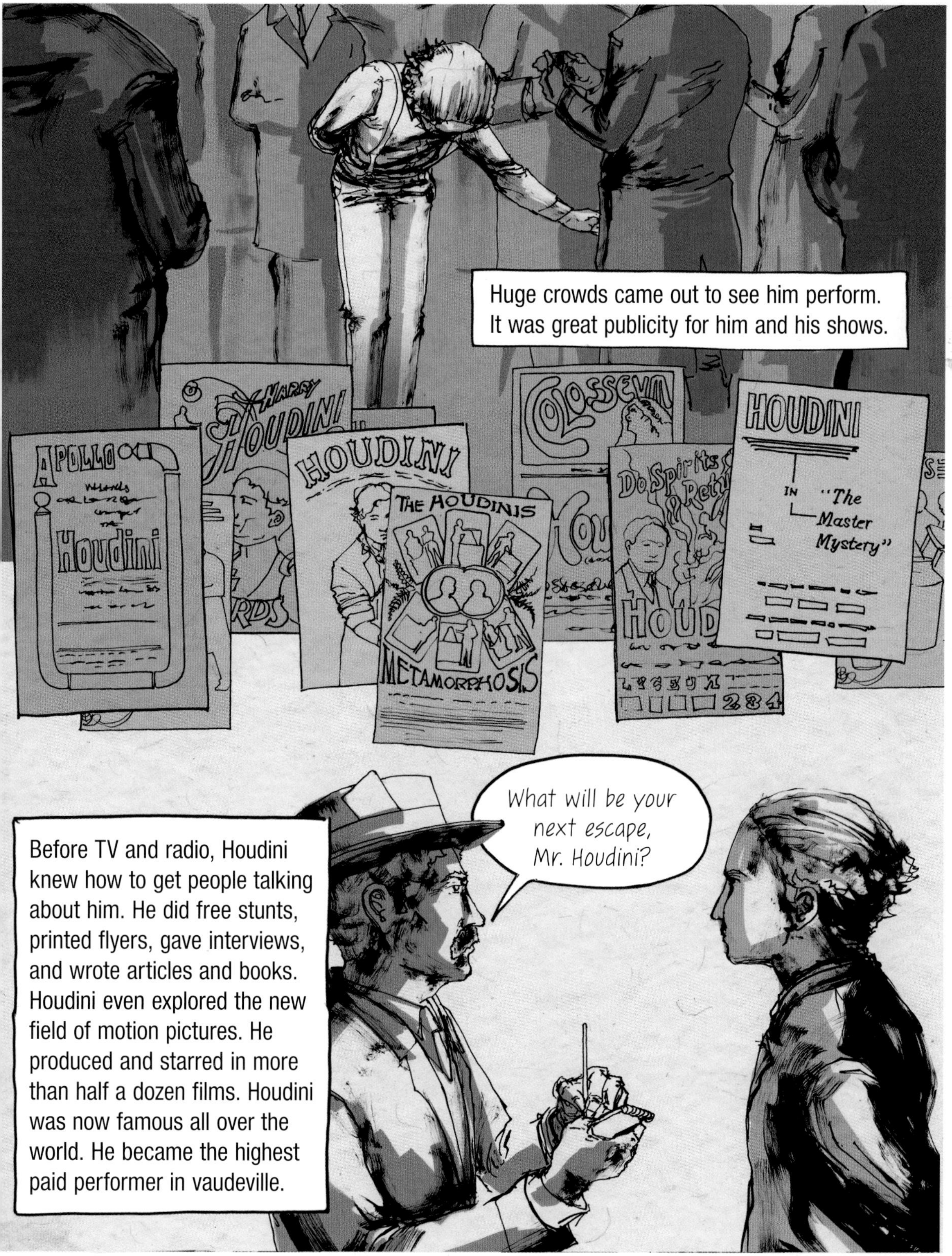
Huge crowds came out to see him perform. It was great publicity for him and his shows.
APOLLO
Houdini
HARRY
HOUDINI
HOUDINI
THE HOUDINIS
METAMORPHOSIS
COLOSSEVM
HOUDINI
IN "The Master Mystery"
What will be your next escape, Mr. Houdini?
Before TV and radio, Houdini knew how to get people talking about him. He did free stunts, printed flyers, gave interviews, and wrote articles and books. Houdini even explored the new field of motion pictures. He produced and starred in more than half a dozen films. Houdini was now famous all over the world. He became the highest paid performer in vaudeville.

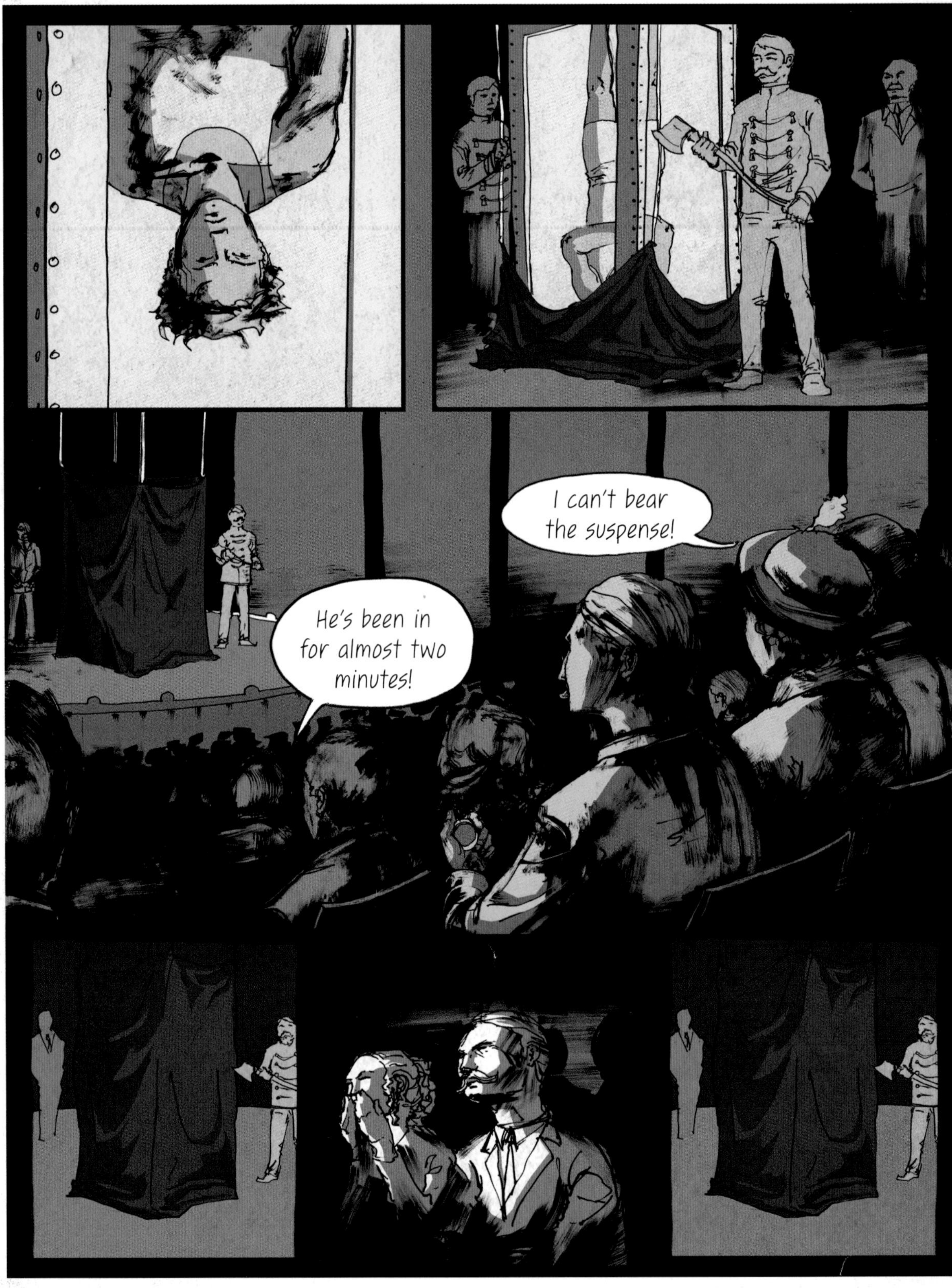

I can't bear the suspense!
He's been in for almost two minutes!

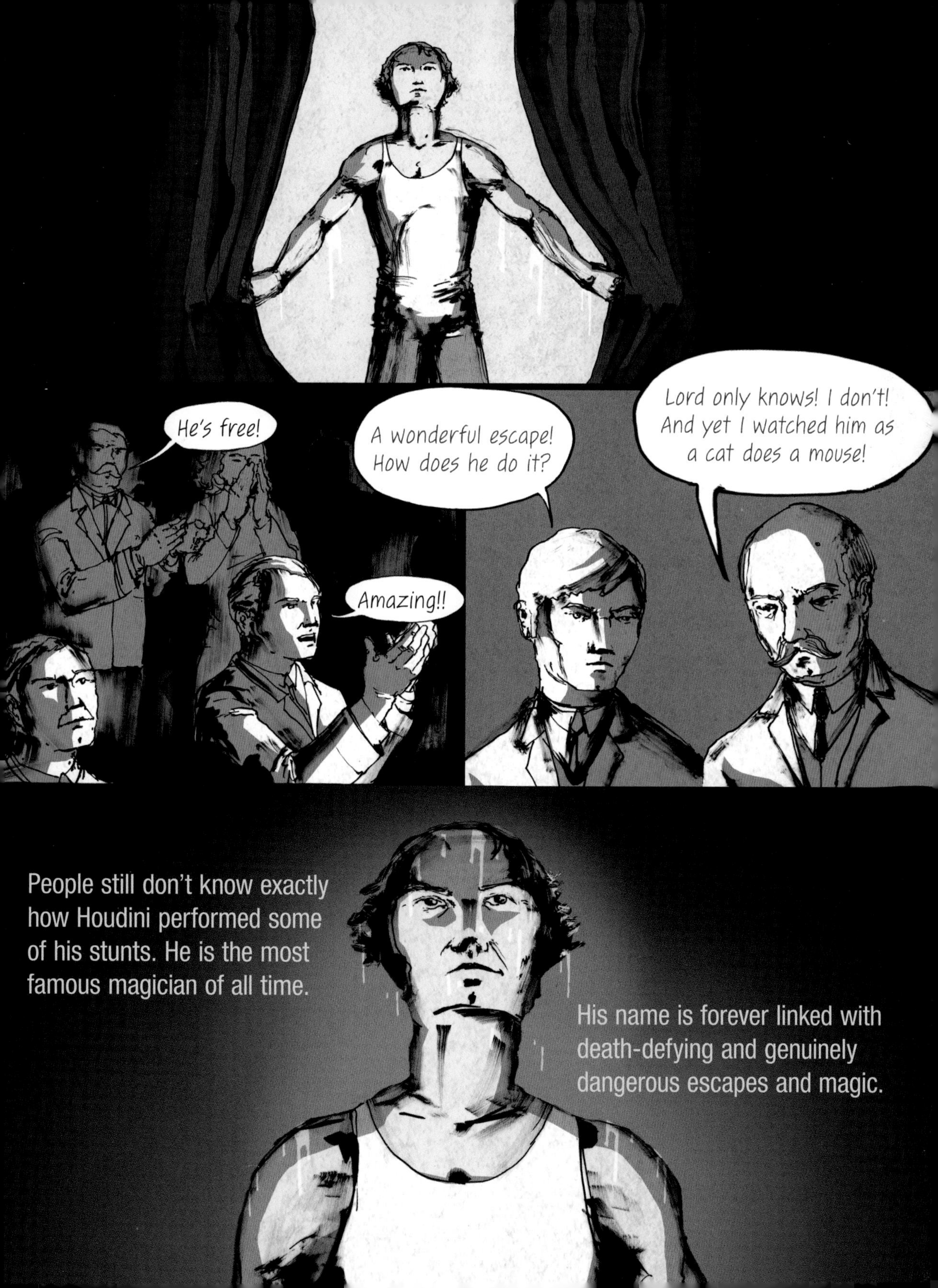
He's free!
Amazing!!
A wonderful escape! How does he do it?
Lord only knows! I don't! And yet I watched him as a cat does a mouse!
People still don't know exactly how Houdini performed some of his stunts. He is the most famous magician of all time.
His name is forever linked with death-defying and genuinely dangerous escapes and magic.

THE LEGACY OF HOUDINI

Houdini continued performing his amazing escapes throughout his career. Later in his life, he also exposed spiritualists as frauds.

Spiritualists claimed they could contact the dead. But Houdini could easily spot the tricks spiritualists used during their séances. He saw how they took advantage of people's grief. Unlike spiritualists, Houdini didn't pretend to have any magical powers. He wanted to be admired for his creativity, courage, and strength. He used part of his act to expose these types of swindlers.

In 1926 Houdini entertained some college students in his dressing room before a performance in Montréal, Quebec, Canada. One student asked about Houdini's physical strength. Was it true that Houdini could take body hits without being hurt? Never one to refuse a challenge, Houdini agreed to be hit. Before Houdini could prepare himself, the student began punching him hard in the abdomen.

Houdini was in great pain, but performed that evening. He then traveled to his next tour stop in Detroit, Michigan. A doctor examined him and saw signs of appendicitis. But Houdini insisted on performing again on October 24. It was his last performance.

The next afternoon, Houdini's burst appendix was removed. But the rupture had caused a serious infection. Part of Houdini's legend is that the student's blows killed him. But it is likely that Houdini was already suffering from appendicitis when he was punched.

Houdini died on Halloween in 1926 at the age of 52. Before he died, he told his wife that if he could reach her beyond the grave, he would. She held annual séances for 10 years without Houdini appearing. Even today, magicians traditionally hold séances to try to contact Houdini. Almost 100 years after his death, Houdini's legend remains very much alive.

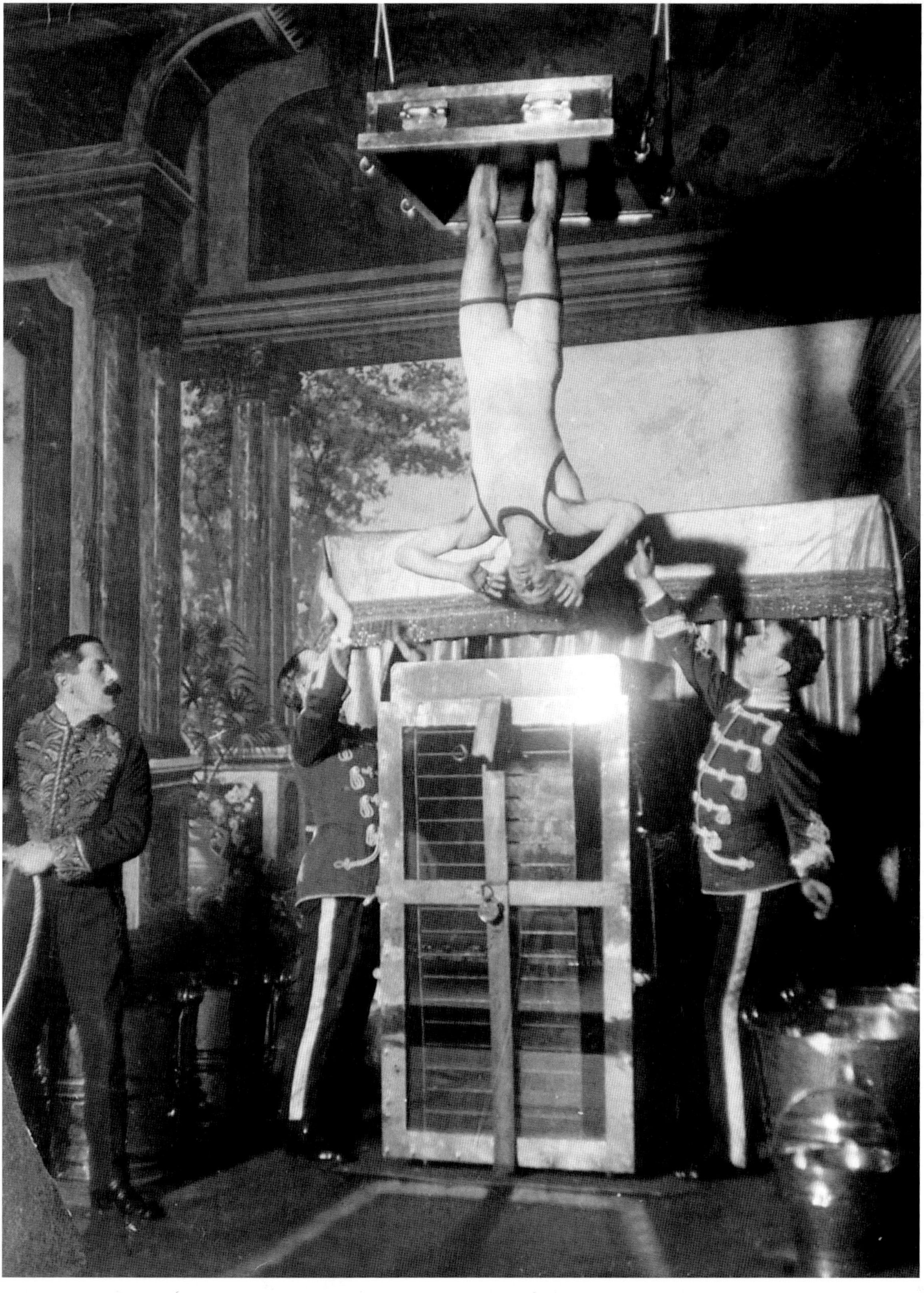

GLOSSARY

accusation (AK-yoo-ZAY-shuhn)—a claim that someone has done something wrong

appendicitis (uh-pen-duh-SY-tuhss)—a disease of the appendix

appendix (uh-PEN-diks)—a bodily organ attached to the large intestine

blacksmith (BLAK-smith)—someone who makes and mends things made of iron

boiler (BOY-luhr)—a tank that boils water to produce steam

death-defying (DETH-di-FYE-ing)—having to do with actions that risk death

fraud (FRAWD)—a person or thing that is not what it seems or is represented to be

illusion (i-LOO-zhuhn)—something that appears to be real but isn't

manacle (MAN-i-cul)— to chain or handcuff by the wrists or ankles

metamorphosis (meht-uh-MOR-fuh-siss)—any complete or great change in appearance, form, or character

publicize (PUHB-luh-size)—to make something known to as many people as possible

séance (SAY-onss)—a meeting at which people try to make contact with the dead

spiritualist (SPIHR-uh-choo-uhl-ist)—someone who claims to be able to communicate with spirits of the dead

stock (STOK)—an adjustable wooden structure with holes for locking a person's feet or hands

straitjacket (STRAYT-jak-it)—a strong garment with long sleeves that can be tied together to confine a person's arms

stunt (STUHNT)—an act that shows great skill or daring

supernatural (soo-pur-NACH-ur-uhl)—something that cannot be given an ordinary explanation

swindler (SWIND-luhr)—someone who cheats someone else out of money or property

vaudeville (VOD-vill)—a stage show that may include comedy, music, magic, and stunts

MILK CAN ESCAPE

30

READ MORE

Carlson, Laurie M. *Harry Houdini for Kids: His Life and Adventures with 21 Magic Tricks and Illusions.* For Kids. Chicago: Chicago Review Press, 2009.

Piehl, Janet. *Harry Houdini.* History Maker Bios. Minneapolis, Minn.: Lerner Publications, 2009.

Selznick, Brian. *The Houdini Box.* New York : Atheneum Books for Young Readers, 2008.

HANDCUFF KING

UNDERWATER BOX ESCAPE

INTERNET SITES

FactHound offers a safe, fun way to find Internet sites related to this book. All of the sites on FactHound have been researched by our staff.

Here's all you do:

Visit *www.facthound.com*

Type in this code: 9781429654746

INDEX

AMERICAN GRAPHIC

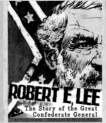
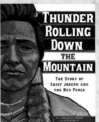